Published 2017 by Sivananda Yoga Vedanta Dhanwantari Ashram
Neyyar Dam
Kerala 695572
India

ISBN: 978-1541181670

Names and identifying details of contributors have been changed where requested.

Cover art by Pierre Duruflé

Ashram

Hazel Manuel

Sivananda Yoga Vedanta Dhanwantari Ashram,
Kerala, India

Introduction

By Nataraj, Director of the Sivananda Yoga Vedanta Dhanwantari Ashram

A very warm welcome to the Sivananda Yoga Vedanta Dhanwantari Ashram.

The Ashram was founded by Swami Vishnudevananda in 1978 and from very small beginnings, when yoga was practised only by the few, it has grown into a thriving and internationally-renowned centre for the teaching of classical yoga.

Swami Vishnudevananda was a direct disciple of the modern-day saint Swami Sivananda and spent his life bringing yoga, in an accessible form, to the world. He founded the International Sivananda Yoga Vedanta Centre organisation in 1959 of which this Ashram is a part.

This beautiful little book, written by one of our guests as an offering to the Ashram, is intended to give you a guide and overview of life in the Ashram—what you may experience from your stay here. We hope that by reading it you will, in the words of one of the guests, "try everything, and don't worry if you don't like it all at first. Just give it a go." and that like another visitor, you will discover that "Yoga gives energy and health, but it has also helped me to realise that being still and silent is possible."

We invite you with full heart to stay at our Ashram and know that your time with us will be enriching and rewarding, bringing renewed peace, joy and vitality to your life.

Leaving

Yoga is the art of right living. Yoga is a system of education not only of the body and the mind or the intellect, but also of the inner spirit. Yoga is a journey into the inner Self.

Swami Sivananda

People young and old journey from all over the world leaving behind their everyday lives to spend time at the Sivananda Yoga Vedanta Dhanwantari Ashram. Why? Who are the many thousands of people each year, who come to this quiet place of learning and devotion, nestled deep in the hills of Kerala? What are the reasons why people of all ages and from all walks of life, make the journey to the Ashram?

Expectation is in the air as you pass through Reception. You can see it in their faces, you can sense it in the way they are absorbing the sights and sounds, these new arrivals at the Ashram. Some have flown in directly from far-away continents, their first time to India and all it has to offer, others are travel-worn India-devotees, exploring one aspect of the vast panoply of life with which this sub-continent pulsates. Some are spiritual seekers, others yoga aficionados, some ashram-hoppers, others returnees and yet others indefinable in their purpose for being here. But all are expectant. Different ages, a mass of different cultures and as many walks of life as nationalities.

Many thousands come each year to experience whatever life has to offer them here in this sacred spot in south India. And what do they find? What do they go away with? What do they understand and love? What do they baulk against? What do they learn?

One of the striking aspects of Ashram life is that it is a disciplined environment involving a set routine that yogis are expected to observe. When to get up and when to go to bed are prescribed by the daily schedule as are meal times, *satsang*, meditation and all the other activities. On Fridays are yogis free to follow their own schedule, although if they remain within the Ashram, they attend morning and evening *satsang*. The daily routine was established by Swami Vishnudevananda, who, following instructions from his teacher Swami Sivananda, revitalised yoga both in the West and in the land of its birth.

Spiritual discipline may be described as observing those behaviours which help our spiritual growth – a path which if followed leads to spiritual liberation. All of the activities prescribed in the Ashram schedule, from morning meditation, through to evening *satsang* are designed to help us move beyond our everyday mind-set of reacting to our thoughts, feelings and emotions, towards a more spiritually-enlightened state. The pursuit of such a state requires dedication, self-control and a willingness to set aside what we think we know about ourselves and the world around us. By following the Ashram's teachings and practices we develop a physically, emotionally and spiritually healthier life-style.

Whatever has brought them, travellers here are likely to arrive at Trivandrum – now known as Thiruvananthapuram, its ancient Indian name. 'City of Lord Anantha' in the local language, Malayalam. The heart of Lord Anantha - the serpent of the Hindu deity Vishnu - always delights in virtue, so it is said. Ninety kilometres short of India's southern-most tip, the city is Kerala state's richly sensuous, typically chaotic capital. The serpent, alive with the sights, sounds and smells of people, scooters, rickshaws, cows and sandy-coloured dogs all vying for space in the busy streets lies ready to receive. If you've arrived by plane, you'll have skirted the Arabian Sea, sparkling in a wide sweep to the north and south. You'll also have seen Trivandrum itself, coiled around and atop its nine hills. Soon enough you'll plunge into the scorching-hot mayhem that typifies Indian cities the country over.

Alex is a 26 year-old geology student and a first time visitor to India from his native Spain. "I wouldn't describe myself as religious," he says. "But I know there's more to life than we think." Keen to learn more about Indian philosophy, Alex will spend two weeks at the Ashram. "I know I'll be learning yoga as well as philosophy," he says. "I am very much looking forward to it."

The heat and the commotion Alex experienced on leaving the relatively tranquil, air-conditioned airport were breath-taking. "The temperature must have been 38 degrees" he says. "I was expecting that, but I was surprised by the hustle and bustle of the taxi and rickshaw drivers, touting for business. A Swedish lady told me about the pre-paid taxi booth, where you're given a ticket with a set price. I was very happy – I really just wanted to get to the Ashram."

Those who arrive by train or bus will likely already have been initiated into the haggling tactics of Indian road transport but will nonetheless need to decide how to complete the onward journey to the Ashram. It is possible to get a bus, as Maria, a 31 year- old nurse from Germany did. "The bus station is just across the street from the train station," she says. "The Ashram is close to Neyyar Dam which is where the bus finishes, so it's really easy and definitely the cheapest way to go."

Maria took a walk in the city before getting the bus. "It was crazy and wonderful," she says, "Loud and busy. And well worth it." It isn't Maria's first time in India. "I was here three years ago. What I love are the contradictions. Yes there are problems, but then you smell the incense, see the smiling children... everyone wearing stunning bright colours... I just love it."

Whether you've already spent some time in Trivandrum, or are keen to get to the Ashram, having decided upon your mode of transport, it's time to leave behind the confines of the city and head east. The Ashram is less than thirty kilometres away, and if you take a bus, taxi or a rickshaw, the journey will be a little over an hour on winding roads dotted with busy little towns, colourful villas and ramshackle villages.

"It was the first I'd seen of India apart from the airport," Alex says. "After we left Trivandrum, the traffic thinned out and we started heading uphill through palm forests, along all these little lanes. The driver was amazing, hurtling round pot-holes and brilliantly-painted Indian lorries. There was a religious festival happening along the way with drumming, people chanting – much of it projected over loudspeakers. It was very powerful. In one village we stopped at a chai stand and had a cup of tea while I watched. It was awesome."

Neyyar Dam... a tiny hamlet named for the nearby irrigation dam, nestles in the foothills of the Western Ghats, the mountain range that snakes its way down India's western flank. Mount Agasthya rises to the north of the hamlet, the River Neyyar flowing into a mist-shrouded lake. The bus shudders to a stop by a big hoarding displaying the name 'Sivananda Ashram'. First time visitors are no doubt relieved to know that they are close. The twenty-minute walk is up a steep hill to the Ashram itself...but whether it's your first visit or your fifth, you can't fail to be moved by Kerala's sheer majestic beauty.

"I was dumbstruck," says Maria. "After the city, I never expected such stunning scenery. I just stood there at the top of the hill, drinking in the view of the lake and the trees with the mountains behind..." But she was a little nervous as well. "I came to the Ashram because I'd read about it in a yoga magazine," Maria says "but I didn't know what it would be like. Now that I was actually here, I felt pretty anxious walking up the steps and into the Ashram itself. There were all these people dressed in yellow and white and I could hear chanting coming from somewhere inside. I have to admit, even though I loved being back in India, I wondered what I'd let myself in for...I mean, an Ashram! I had literally no idea what to expect..."

Dawn meditation

Meditation is painful in the beginning but it bestows immortal bliss and supreme joy in the end.

Swami Sivananda

It is 5.30 in the morning, the sun has yet to rise and a bell is ringing somewhere outside. Little by little, the sounds of people rousing themselves from sleep take the place of your dreams and you too lift yourself, perhaps reluctantly from your bed. Outside your room all is dark, the hills beyond the Ashram nothing but black shapes in the distance. You join the others making their way in silence to the big Dhanwantari Hall with its statues and shrines while a deep, repetitive chant intones...Om... Om... Om...

By 6am you have taken your place in the hall which is already full of others, some sleepy, maybe still in their dreams. The chanting stops. The only sounds now are the calling of the birds, beginning their own dawn chorus. You are gently guided into twenty minutes of silent meditation while the day breaks and all around the Ashram nature wakes up. When you open your eyes, you are surprised to see that the sun has risen, all is bathed in glorious sunshine, the day has begun.

The chanting begins again, but this time it is a *bhajan* – a devotional call and response chant beginning with what will become the familiar *Jaya Ganesha* chant.

8

The words are not familiar, you don't know what they mean, but you do your best to follow along from the chant-book someone has passed you. This is *satsang*, the twice- daily gathering of all— staff, students and guests alike— that takes place morning and evening at the Ashram. The chanting, meditation and a short discourse on yoga philosophy open and close each day.

Rasida is 32 years old and is the enthusiastic head of marketing for a Delhi-based export company. She is thinking of training as a yoga teacher in her spare time and has come to the Ashram to explore the teachings.

"It was a little strange to begin with," she says. "I had never stayed at an Ashram before." Rasida found the 5.30 am starts a real challenge at first. "It was hard," she says. "I found it difficult to get up so early and I didn't think I'd adapt. But I quickly became used to it. It's much cooler at that time of day, so in fact it makes sense to make the most of it."

The majority of people who stay at the Ashram sleep in one of the seven single-sex dormitories, where they share living space – a bed plus shower area with up to thirty others. Rasida doesn't mind communal living. "I'm an extrovert and I'm from a large family. I like being around other people."

"I slept badly at first," says Sue from Devon, in the UK. "I'm 56 and hadn't slept in a dormitory for a very long time." Having lost her mother who she had been intensely caring for, Sue decided to visit India for a second time, having come the first time with her son's father in the late 1980s. This time, her son – now 27, is travelling with her. Sue has been an irregular yoga practitioner for a number

9

of years, and having heard about the Ashram from a friend, felt that now was a good time to come. "I felt insecure to begin with," she says. But her anxiety didn't last. "I feel far more relaxed now. I appreciate the fact of being able to come here. It's a very special experience. Being at the Ashram has renewed my desire for a daily yoga and meditation practice at home."

Mark is originally from Canada but is living in California where he is studying acupuncture. He came to India to backpack with a group of friends and decided to spend a few days at the Ashram alone before meeting up with them again. "It's great travelling with friends," he says. "But you do need a break. A girl we met in Kovalam told us about this place and I thought I'd check it out."

Mark also found the 5.30am starts a challenge. "I'm not one of those who sleeps in all morning, but man, getting up when it's still dark...that's tough!" He laughs as he describes being woken by one of the Ashram volunteer staff every day of his stay. "They don't let you sleep in," he says. "The early start is compulsory so I just told myself to go with it."

A lot of the people who stay at the Ashram question the early morning start. But there is a reason for the pre-dawn wake-up call. Swami Sivananda explains that the period of time just before dawn is the best time to meditate. Visitors to the Ashram are taught that regular meditation enables the mind to become clear, helping us to better understand ourselves and our relationship to the world. Through specific techniques which are taught at the Ashram, meditation can help us to be aware of the present and of the choices we have in our lives, rather than constantly living in the past or in the future. This awareness connects us with a more peaceful reality which we are unlikely to find unless we discipline our minds through meditation. With regular practice this can lead to a life of wisdom and peace.

Rasida already had a daily meditation practice before coming to the Ashram. "Meditation for me is a powerful way to still my mind and let what is unimportant go. That helps me to keep focused throughout the day, and the work I do benefits – I'm able to remain calm and grounded, no matter what is going on. The practice makes me a better decision maker. Here we meditate sitting cross-legged on the floor - that wasn't so easy for me initially," she says. Nonetheless, Rasida is making progress. The reason for sitting cross-legged is to stabilise the body and to allow the energy to flow freely. "That made sense to me and I persevered. I could barely do a minute of meditation at first without having to change position. Now I can sit with my legs crossed throughout the practice."

Mark is new to meditation and isn't sure he's fully grasped the technique. "I'm not sure I understand all the teachings yet," he says. "But there is a logic behind everything we do. We're taught that in the meditation we focus the mind using a mantra as an aid." A mantra is a sound with mystical properties which is repeated over and over. Mark says that keeping the mind focused is impossible for him at this point, but he repeats the universal mantra 'OM' during meditations. "Even if you can't even focus on repeating the mantra, having that quiet time, trying not to get distracted by your thoughts - is a great way to set yourself up for the day. I think we miss that in our lives, our thoughts are always rushing from one thing to the next. I definitely plan when I get back home on getting up twenty minutes earlier to take a quiet moment before starting the day."

Meet me by the Tea Tree

Individual peace paves the way for world
peace. The attainment of inner calm is the
greatest work you can do for humanity.

Swami Sivananda

At the foot of the steps leading up to the
Dhanwantari Hall, there is a little open space. To one side
there is a clear view down a tree-lined valley to the
temple-topped mountains beyond. To the other lies a
well-tended lawn. Statues of Hindu deities Vishnu, Radha
and Krishna watch over the comings and goings while two
tall trees stand sentinel within the little clearing. It is here
that thirsty yogis gather twice each day to drink tea, chat
with friends or simply gaze out over the valley.

Here the daily rhythm has its own logic. Following
the morning meditation, tea is served at 7.30am before
the first yoga asana session of the day. Meals are served
after the classes so that the stomach isn't too full for the
energetic movements and postures and so breakfast-cum-
brunch is served at 10am. So instead of eating an early
breakfast, the yogis drink tea.

Tea-time is great for people-watching. The more
extroverted stand in the middle of the clearing, making
new friends and chatting over their tea, while those who
are less so gravitate towards the edge where they can turn
away from the hubbub and focus instead on the view.
Ashram life involves being with other people much of the

13

time. For some, this is a great opportunity to meet new friends, share experiences and enjoy the social aspects of communal living. For others the challenge is how to maintain a still center when one is amongst other guests.

Bonita is a 37-year-old Indian youth worker from London. It is her first visit to the Ashram and she has come here following mental health issues which she says have made it difficult for her to work and function normally. Her aim in coming here is to remove herself from her situation and to work on her mind and body before entering into therapy back home. Bonita enjoys the yoga asana classes, and although not previously a regular yoga practitioner, feels that she is making good physical progress. "The teacher is very good," she says. "She makes me feel like I can push myself and this is a big achievement for me. I always feel great after the sessions, even if I've struggled with the postures."

But Bonita has sometimes found the Ashram routine difficult, particularly *satsang* and meditation. "Sometimes I feel I cannot connect to the chanting and I find the meditation hard. But I have made progress, and I am certainly not giving up."

Bonita has noticed an interesting change in her behaviour. "The best part about being at the Ashram has been meeting people from all walks of life," she says. "Everyone is on their own journey. And perhaps because I'm away from home and the people I usually associate with, I find that I'm able to be more expressive – I can be more open with people about myself, my feelings and my thoughts."

Pam is a 35-year-old nurse from Ireland who is also living in London. She too enjoys meeting new people and has made many new friends at the Ashram. It is Pam's second visit. She had never done Sivananda yoga before, but a friend who did the yoga teachers' training course at the Ashram recommended her to come. Pam enjoyed her first stay at the Ashram so much that she decided to return. "I'm impressed that people follow the programme so willingly," she says. "I think it's because we are treated with kindness."

Pam says that she sometimes finds the second asana class of the day a challenge because by then the weather is very hot and she is often tired. "I always feel energised after though, and I'm always glad I went," she says. Having struggled with the chanting during her first visit, Pam now finds it uplifting and practises at home, especially if she is feeling low. She has also started attending yoga classes and *satsang* at the London Sivananda Yoga Centre. "The asana practice and the meditation make me feel more centred," she says. Pam advises new-comers to have an open mind. "Try everything, and don't worry if you don't like it all at first. Just give it a go."

Tomas seeks opportunities to be alone. A 53-year-old artist from Mexico, he was surprised at how many people stay at the Ashram at any one time. "There must be nearly three hundred people here at the moment," he says. Swami Sivananda talks about the benefits of silence, which he says are 'incalculable'. He teaches that in order to achieve a state of lasting happiness and peace, we must first know how to calm the mind. By turning the mind's concentration inward, upon the inner Self, we can deepen the experience of perfect concentration, thereby finding a profound sense of inner peace.

"It's something I need to learn," Tomas says. "to find my own silence, even when I'm surrounded by people. It's easy to feel still and connected to the universe and nature when alone up a mountain or on a deserted beach. But where is the challenge in that?" Tomas heard about the Ashram while working as a volunteer teacher in Tamil Nadu, just east of Kerala, and, spiritual growth being the focus of his journey, decided to visit. "I was led to the Ashram in order to learn certain spiritual lessons," he says. "The ability to maintain inner silence no matter how busy the environment, is perhaps the biggest lesson for me here. It's hard, but it's often the more difficult lessons that are the most worthwhile. I'm learning."

Yoga: more than just stretching

Yoga brings peace and lasting happiness. You can have calmness of mind at all times by the practice of yoga.

Swami Sivananda

"I thought the people I'd meet at the Ashram would all be mystical hippies!" Henny is a 21-year-old theology student from the UK and had never stayed at an Ashram before. She had planned nine weeks in India and had been travelling and doing volunteer work as part of her gap-year experience. She read about the Ashram in the Lonely Planet Guide and thought it would be good to see what it was like. Henny had never meditated or practised yoga before, but is a sports aficionado. She felt that following the Ashram's daily schedule would be an active and healthy conclusion to her stay in India.

Henny soon realised that the Ashram's inhabitants were not all 'mystical hippies' but a wide mix, some of whom she has made strong connections with. "I feel honoured to have met such people," she says. "None of my friends at home have interests like yoga, but I've met people here that I am so happy to know."

Henny has realised that yoga is more than just the asanas. She says that the communal-living aspect of

Ashram life is no problem but that she hasn't yet grasped the idea of meditation. Although she is new to the Ashram teachings and way of life though, Henny has fully appreciated learning the yoga asana practice. At the Ashram, beginner and intermediate classes are offered as well as gentle classes for people who need a softer session. Henny joined the beginner's class. "I felt very nervous at first," she says. "I panicked because I was stiff and inflexible and could not do the postures well." That soon changed, and Henny says that she felt the physical benefits of the sessions even after the first day.

The Sivananda system of classical hatha yoga was designed by Swami Vishnudevananda, from his teacher Swami Sivananda, and uses a set sequence of twelve postures introduced by the sun salutation, a powerful yoga warm-up. The physical and mental benefits of asana practice are enormous and wide-ranging and include helping to tone the nervous system, improve circulation, release tension, and increase flexibility.

Asana practice is carried out twice each day at the Ashram, at 8am and 3.30pm. Each session lasts for almost two hours and begins with pranayama—the yogic breathing techniques to control the breath in order to cleanse and nourish the physical body and calm the mind. Ashram visitors are taught that proper breathing techniques increase vitality and improve brain power. Following the pranayama and asana practice, each yoga session ends with a period of deep relaxation during which students learn to completely let go of mind and body.

By the end of her first week, Henny was feeling stronger, healthier and more flexible. She was surprised that after each session, despite the hard physical work, she felt energised rather than exhausted. "Don't be daunted if you are new to yoga," Henny advises. "The teachers are lovely and will help you as much as you need."

Vestna has been practising yoga for the past twenty years. Originally from Croatia, she now lives in Vienna, Austria, where she works in the theatre business. Vestna typically attends classes at the Vienna Sivananda Yoga Centre two or three times each week. "I wanted to come to India to experience yoga in its country of origin," she says. Like Henny, Vestna is a sports lover, and she sees yoga as an important part of her life. She values the physical health benefits that yoga brings, feeling her body becoming stronger and more flexible. She also enjoys the environment in which the classes are carried out. "It is very clean and green here at the Ashram," she says. "I love the fresh air and the nature. I swim in the lake every day. All this helps with stress."

Yoga asanas are designed to develop more than just the physical body, and when performed slowly and meditatively can also strengthen and pacify the mind, helping us to deal with life's situations with awareness and calm, and to experience a sense of well-being. By combining asana practice with meditation and other spiritual practices, yoga helps us to find peace and happiness within, which the Ashram teaches, is our true nature.

Vestna is aware of these deeper benefits. "Yoga gives energy and health, but it has also helped me to realise that being still and silent is possible," she says. "Even here, surrounded by other people, I can find a silent place of peace inside myself." Vestna feels that along with the physical practice of yoga, she is influenced by the spiritual ideas behind it. She grew up with communism and atheism but is open to the teachings of Swami Sivananda. "Yoga takes away fear because it teaches you acceptance," she says. "When we see the bad things that happen in life, we realise how lucky we are to have this paradise."

Selfless acts done with kindness

Put your heart, mind, and soul into even your smallest acts. This is the secret of success.

Swami Sivananda

'Meet by the Tea Tree at 11am, to be given your karma yoga.' The morning announcements after *satsang* always include this instruction, and new arrivals gather under the tree to be assigned their allotted task. Everyone who stays is expected to engage in selfless service – to contribute in some way to the smooth running of the Ashram. This certainly ensures that the dormitories are clean, food is served, and that rooms and halls are prepared for yoga, lectures and *satsang*.

"There were a few of us waiting by the Tea Tree to be given our karma yoga," says Norris, a 47-year-old writer from Denmark. "I wasn't sure what karma yoga was. I thought yoga was just the exercises. But I now know that the postures are just one aspect."

Norris had been asked to come to India to deliver some lectures at a university and came to the Ashram to relax for a few days before returning to Denmark. He is a natural early-riser and so the 5.30am starts have posed no problem for him and he is tolerant of the chattier people in

21

his dormitory. "Young people are often more exuberant," he says. "I was probably like that when I was in my twenties." And he is finding the meditation and chanting interesting. "I like the communality of it all," he says. "Everyone sitting together singing. I enjoy it." However, Ashram life isn't quite as Norris had expected. "I didn't realise the karma yoga and all the other things were compulsory," he laughs. "I honestly thought I'd be doing a bit of gentle yoga in the mornings, and relaxing by the lake with a good book all afternoon!" Norris was asked to help serve the meals for his karma yoga. "At first I was a little resistant," he says. "I've joined in with everything, but I didn't come here to be a waiter." But Norris has changed his view. "Everyone has their own job to do and after a while I came to enjoy mine. I've realised that with so many people to feed, they need some help." He also enjoys the spirit of co-operation that karma yoga engenders. "We are all working for a common purpose, " he says.

The idea behind performing karma yoga is not only practical. The word *karma* means 'action' in Sanskrit and is an important aspect of the yogic way of life. Swami Sivananda teaches us that selfless work, done in a spirit of giving for no personal gain and with no thought for our own interests or desires, is a powerful way to evolve spiritually. He advises us to 'speak a helpful word, give a cheering smile, do a kind act, serve a little, wipe the tears of one who is in distress.'

Florence is from Dijon in France and has come to the Ashram following the break-up of a long-term relationship. "I needed to be in a place of peace," she says. "I was going around in circles at home, obsessing about my ex-partner. My self-esteem was failing and I was falling into some self-destructive behaviours. My sister suggested I come to the Ashram. She goes to yoga classes at the Paris Sivananda Yoga Centre and visited the Ashram a few years ago. I came in order to heal and to focus on something other than my own hurt." Florence—a 29-year-old translator—says that the karma yoga is helping. "I wash the toilets and the showers," she laughs. "It's not very glamorous, but I put all my love into it, knowing that the other women in my dormitory appreciate clean conditions when they take their shower."

Florence says that cleaning toilets isn't going to heal her broken heart, but that the attitude of selfless service is helping her to shift her perspective. "I've been here for ten days and I feel stronger already," she says. "I see a world here that doesn't revolve around obsessing about ourselves and our lives. I think the idea of karma yoga is healthy, especially for people in the West, where the tendency is to be self-centred. I'm planning to do some volunteer work when I go back home."

'Please eat in silence!'

Mother Nature has demonstrated her marvellous skill and power in cultivating these wonderful vegetables for her children.

Swami Sivananda

Many of the people who come to stay at the Ashram are asked as their karma yoga to help serve the food. Meals are served twice each day, brunch at 10am and dinner at 6pm. *Thali* plates full of freshly-cooked south Indian-style rice, vegetables and pulses are served in a large dining hall where after an initial prayer yogis eat in silence seated cross-legged on rush mats. There is also the Health Hut—the Ashram's version of a café—where yogis come to socialise with glasses of fruit smoothies, ginger, lemon and honey drinks, fresh fruit and nut plates and other delicious offerings, under a coconut-thatched roof which covers wooden tables and benches. The soft lighting and the murmur and hum of conversation creates an ambience that is inviting and relaxing.

All the food at the Ashram, whether served at meal-times or at the Health Hut is based on the principles of a yogic diet. Everything offered is *sattvic*—pure—locally-produced, vegetarian, and consisting only of foods that are easily digested and which promote good health to the individual and the environment. Meat, fish, eggs, onions, garlic, mushrooms and very hot spices are not considered to be *sattvic* and so are not eaten. Visitors to the Ashram are taught that a *sattvic* diet creates a healthy body and, just as importantly, a healthy mind.

"The food at the Ashram was not what I expected," says Karl. "I'm a big guy and I need a lot to sustain me especially when I'm so active. I honestly thought I'd die of starvation when I saw only two meals per day on the schedule." Karl, 33 years old and from Finland is a perpetual traveller.   "I've seen a lot of the planet," he says. He is working his way around the world giving English lessons, returning home to Finland from time to time to catch up with his family and work for the money for his next adventure. Karl flew to Delhi ten weeks ago and has been making his way down from north to south. He decided to stay in an Ashram as part of his India experience. "I wanted to do everything India has to offer," he says, "including an Ashram – I will stay a while."

Karl has a great love of food. "For me that's one of the best things about travel – trying all the different cuisines." One of his concerns about the Ashram diet was what he took to be a lack of protein. But he was pleased to find that what is served gives him plenty of energy. "The protein comes in the beans and lentils and rice," he says. "And there are lots of fresh vegetables – we are offered as much as we can eat. We do not go hungry. The brunches and the dinners here are good. I'm not a vegetarian – with my lifestyle you have to eat what you can get. But it's obvious the diet here is healthy."

Gorika had her own concerns about the Ashram diet. "I'm Indian," she says, "I grew up in a village near Trishur as a vegetarian. There's dahl and sambar and rice and all here, but I wanted it to be more spicy."

Gorika is 27 and soon to be married. "I feel strongly about upholding our traditions," she says. "My parents and I felt that this purifying and spiritual experience would affirm my intention to make a good marriage." What she learned in one of the daily lectures has gone some way to appeasing her doubts about the Ashram food. "Different foods have different effects on our mind and our body," she says. "For example, spicy foods like chillies or black pepper have the effect of over-heating us – not just physically but emotionally too. It's more than just what the food tastes like that is of importance."

The yogic diet takes into account the values and teachings of yoga in order to achieve not only physical health, but also spiritual and moral development. Swami Sivananda taught that the mind depends on the subtle essence of food for its formation – the quality of the mind depends on the quality of the food. Eating freshly-prepared, simple vegetarian food allows us to keep the mind calm and to go deeper into our meditation. In addition, not eating meat, fish and eggs adheres to the yogic principle of *ahimsa,* non-harming, and is seen as a more nurturing choice of diet.

To further enhance their spiritual nature, meals are eaten in silence with an attitude of appreciation, to foster focus on the food and gratitude for it. Karl finds eating in silence a real challenge. "I'm a social guy," he says. "And I'm used to meal-times being a time to socialise. Whenever the staff member reminds us to 'please eat in silence', I'm sure he's talking to me!" Gorika, conversely feels frustration when people speak during mealtimes. She feels that the rules are there for a reason and should be respected.

Gorika isn't planning on giving up the foods she loves like chilli, pepper, garlic and onions. But what she has learned about a *sattvic* diet has given her pause for thought. "I do feel calmer," she says. Whether that's the food or the yoga or the meditation I don't know. It's probably a combination of all. But I did buy a cookery book in the Ashram boutique and I'll be trying out a few of the recipes on my new husband."

Dissolving the veils of ignorance and illusion

There is a lesson in everything. There is a lesson in each experience. Learn it and become wise.

Swami Sivananda

David is not the kind of person you'd expect to meet at an Ashram. A 34-year-old teacher from Surrey in the UK, he describes himself as a confirmed atheist. David came to the Ashram along with his girlfriend as part of their travels in India and was very skeptical. When he first arrived, he caught a glimpse of a yoga asana class in progress and immediately thought "oh no, where has she brought me?!" His idea of yoga was that it was gentle stretching for middle-class mums, and of people who visit Ashrams that they must be crazy. "I didn't want to talk to anyone," he says. "I was out of my depth."

Nonetheless, David resolved to give everything a go. He attended the beginners' yoga class and after only a few days could not believe how strong he felt. A keen sportsman back home, David noticed how yoga does not leave him stiff like other sports, despite being far more energetic and challenging than he had imagined. He now sees it as an excellent complement to other sports. "I have one hundred per cent changed my views about yoga," he says. "I'll definitely be carrying on with it after this." And he is impressed with the diet. "I love the food," he says. "I feel so healthy, I've decided to stay off meat for two days a week."

But it wasn't only the yoga and the diet that made an impression on David. "The lectures are my favourite part," he says. "The teachings are really interesting. I found that the ideas challenged me to think about different ways of explaining life. Even if you are a scientist or an atheist, don't dismiss them." There isn't one specific aspect of the teaching that has most inspired David, but rather the idea of considering a new way of understanding life and the self. However, he has found some of the teachings hard to agree with. "I find the idea of *karma* difficult," he says, "especially in relation to past and future lives."

David is referring to the belief in reincarnation – that we have more than one life and that all of our actions have consequences that can span lifetimes. But he does now see a role for spirituality. "The teachings have made me see that at the very least, it does no harm," he says. "I'm far more open to 'crazy people' now!" Part of what persuaded David to take a more open view was the fact of the positive impact the food and the asana practice have had on him. "Since they got those so right," he says, "the rest can't be so wrong."

The Ashram's lecture programme runs on a two-week cycle and covers the five key principles of the teachings of Swami Vishnudevananda—proper exercise (asanas), proper breathing (pranayama), proper relaxation (*savasan*), proper diet (vegetarian) and proper thinking and meditation (*vedanta* and *dhyana*). It also introduces the four classical paths of yoga: karma yoga—selfless acts of kindness, bhakti yoga—the path of devotion, raja yoga—controlling the mind and the body through meditation, and jnana yoga—the yoga of knowledge and wisdom. Jnana yoga is concerned with gaining knowledge of our true nature and in transcending the individual's identification with mind and body. Swami Sivananda said that jnana yoga is 'direct realisation of oneness or unity with the Supreme Being,' which dissolves the veils of ignorance and illusion. The Ashram's lecture programme sets out the practices that can make it possible to know who and what we truly are.

Many of the people who come to the Ashram do so not to gain knowledge and wisdom, but for the yoga asana practice. Some are surprised and perhaps confused by the teachings. Carla, a 29-year-old yoga teacher from New Jersey, America loves the asana sessions. "I hadn't done Sivananda yoga before," she says, "but I really like it. The set sequence of postures helps me to gauge my own progress. It's certainly something I can incorporate into my teaching back home." Carla finds the lectures thought-provoking but admits that she isn't yet ready for all the teachings. "I just want to do yoga," she says. "It's what I came here for. I am not sure I understand the rest." Carla is staying at the Ashram with her friend who is also a yoga teacher. They plan a two-week stay before exploring southern India. "The yoga teachers here are awesome," she says.

Lesley has found something of immense value in the Sivananda teachings. At 53 years old, Lesley, who is originally from Scotland now lives at the Ashram. A series of traumatic events led Lesley into a destructive and unhealthy lifestyle. The Ashram provides a structure which is not only helping her to regain emotional and physical balance, but also through the teachings, to come to terms with all she has lost. "One of the most powerful parts of the teachings here is not to think about the past or the future but to stay focused on the present." Lesley has found that, in spite of her losses, she is able to do this. Consequently, she says that she now feels full of vitality and positive energy. "A spiritual change is taking place in me," she says. "I feel some inner strength."

Jaya Ganesha, Jaya Ganesha!

There is nothing so inspiring, elevating, solacing and delightful as *satsang*. *Satsang* is the greatest of all purifiers and illuminators

Swami Sivananda

Twice each day, morning and evening the entire Ashram community gathers in the Dhanwantari Hall for *satsang*. After the period of silent meditation, the chanting begins with *Jaya Ganesha*, a call and response chant which starts off slowly and grows in pace and energy to a final climactic finish. Cross-legged yogis pick up tambourines, drums and finger cymbals and up to 300 people raise their voices to the daily singing.

The Sanskrit word *satsang* means 'association with the wise'. Typically for followers of a yogic way of life, this means joining with fellow yogis for meditation, devotional practices and a discourse on the philosophy of yoga. *Satsang* is an extremely important aspect of spiritual practice, which energises, builds spiritual community and nurtures spiritual motivation. A key part of *satsang* is the chanting, or *kirtan* following the meditation practice. Mantras are chanted in 'song' form to the accompaniment of harmonium, drum and tambourine. Mantras, according to the yogic tradition, contain powerful, subtle energies which correspond to energies in the body. *Kirtan* is considered to be the easiest way of uplifting the mind, leading to inner silence. If we embrace it openly, *kirtan* connects us to a higher energy within ourselves by clearing away negative emotions and opening the heart.

In spite of this, for those not used to it, *kirtan* can seem the most 'different' part of the daily schedule. The words of the chants initially can be hard to pronounce and to understand for those not familiar with Sanskrit. *Satsang* can be daunting or exhilarating – perhaps for some, both.

Daniel has decided that he needs a career change. At the age of 43, he has his own business consultancy in Leeds in the UK but in spite of his success, feels strongly that he wants to do something more fulfilling. "Call it a mid-life crisis if you like, " he says, smiling. Personal issues have prompted Daniel to come to India for a number of months with the aim of building a firmer spiritual foundation to his life. He feels compatible with the Ashram's teachings and already has a daily meditation practice which he began some time ago in the UK. "I'm enjoying having a 'digital detox'" he says, referring to the Ashram's policy of minimising the use of mobile phones and other devices.

Daniel has made a lot of effort to push himself with those aspects of Ashram life he finds difficult. Dormitory life interrupts his sleep, which he struggles with in any case, and is a challenge in terms of privacy. He finds the chanting a challenge but feels that he is making progress. "I like the style of gentle encouragement here," he says. " I am learning to achieve a more spiritual set of practices in my life."

33

Meruyert enjoys *satsang* very much and says that it gives her a great deal of positive energy. A 28-year-old university administrator from Kazakhstan, Meruyert is staying for twenty days at the Ashram. Her reason for coming is similar to Daniel's. "I came to experience spiritual rejuvenation," she says. Meruyert had been working long hours at her job and was feeling physically and mentally exhausted when she decided to spend some time here. "I feel that India is the centre of spiritual life. I'd been doing yoga but not regularly and I wanted to get into a regular practice. Living in a spiritual way, praying, being vegetarian, which is not easy in Kazakhstan - these are all important to me."

As soon as she arrived at the Ashram, a little unsure and not knowing what to expect, Meruyert heard chanting and immediately felt better. "I felt alone at first," she says. "It seemed that everyone else knew each other. But I decided to go with it and see what happened. I soon started to make friends and feel more at home – especially after the first *satsang*."

Her experiences at the Ashram have made Meruyert determined to make a lifestyle change, especially in relation to her work. Like Daniel, she wants to find an occupation that will have more meaning for her. "I now see how beautiful life can be," she says. Meruyert understands well the fact that people may be confused by some of what happens at the Ashram. "Let everything happen," she advises. "You don't know what it could lead to. Everything is a lesson. Of *satsang*, she suggests that sitting at the front helps you to feel more involved. "For me it's all about positive energy."

After the *kirtan* yogis listen to a short lecture or a reading from the work of either Swami Sivananda or Swami Vishnudevananda. This is followed by *arati* – a short prayer-ritual of respect and gratitude.

The final part of *satsang* before yogis either begin the daily schedule, or go to bed is the taking of *prasad*. In Sanskrit *prasad* means 'a gracious gift' and refers to foods or other offerings to God. At the end of *satsang* these food offerings are distributed to the yogis present, and because they contain God's blessing, bring peace.

"I like the ritual nature of it all," says Pierre, a 52-year-old network engineer from Paris, France. Pierre first visited the Ashram some years ago when he was introduced to it by his partner. Since then he has taken up aspects of what he learned in his home life. "I do yoga at home," he says. "Not every day, but often. And I acknowledge Ganesha each morning before I go to work. Ganesha is the Indian deity who removes obstacles. For me it's not so much about praying, but setting an intention for the day. Acknowledging Ganesha puts me in the frame of mind where I feel strong and able to overcome adversity."

Pierre believes that marking the transitions of the day brings a finer awareness to our daily lives. "Starting and finishing the day in spiritual mindfulness is a good way to remind ourselves that there is more to life than our day-to-day superficial concerns," he says.

A spiritual discipline

Serve, Love, Give, Purify, Meditate, Realise

Swami Sivananda

Both Swami Sivananda and Swami Vishnudevananda, following the classical tradition of spiritual teaching, instructed their students to follow a disciplined life. They knew that any practice, whether it was asanas, positive thinking, meditation or any of the myriad *sadhanas* (spiritual practices) within the tradition, required continual sustained effort. And for this reason the daily schedule in the Ashram follows a structure in which all guests partake. The body, the mind and the soul are nurtured and after only a few days there is reinvigoration and rejuvenation on all levels.

Olympia is originally from Switzerland but at 41 years old now lives in Uruguay where she and her partner lead a quiet life focusing on their spiritual development. Olympia was drawn by the nature of Ashram life. She came here with her mother, who has been many times before, in order to find peace and healing in their relationship. "We needed to reconnect," she says. "I felt that the Ashram would be a safe environment in which to work on our relationship." Olympia felt awkward and shy at first, but by her third day had 'begun to land.' Talking to others, she realised that many of the people she was meeting all had a common goal – to learn and to develop and this helped her to feel more relaxed. By her fourth day she had begun to feel the positive effects of the asana practice, feeling more supple, invigorated and light. "Feeling the change in my body has made me feel stronger and more confident," she says.

Olympia had planned to stay at the Ashram for two weeks but has decided to stay longer, possibly even to undergo the yoga teacher training course offered here. "Healing has happened in my relationship with my mother," she says. "I believe that this is specifically related to being in the Ashram environment. Because of this and because of the cleansing of mind and body I feel we are in a clearer position to work things out. Being together in this context has helped us to take a big step forward."

Maya, who is 23 had been attending yoga asana classes and *satsang* at the Sivananda Yoga Centre in Tel Aviv, Israel, where she is from and so was familiar with many aspects of the programme. Before coming to the Ashram, she had been travelling in India with her father and had decided that it was time for a change. She heard about the Ashram from someone they met on their travels and, having missed yoga while travelling, left her father to explore Kerala alone while she spent some time here. "I was struck by the size and the beauty of the place," she says. "I felt good energy straight away."

Already being familiar with satsang and meditation, Ashram life isn't completely strange for Maya. But she does sometimes feel restricted. "Having to go to *satsang* when I'm tired is a little testing," she says. However, she does see reason to comply. "We can go deeper spiritually if we participate in everything," she says. So far Maya has been at the Ashram for three weeks and in spite of the discipline, intends to stay longer.

Arriving

Do not brood over your past mistakes and failures as this will only fill your mind with grief, regret and depression. Do not repeat them in the future.

Swami Sivananda

In chapter one, we met Alex – a geology student from Spain, and Maria, a German nurse. Both came with hopes and expectations for their time at the Ashram - Alex with the aim of learning more about Indian philosophy and Maria because she was intrigued by an article she had read in a yoga magazine. We left Alex excited to arrive, and Maria nervous, uncertain, and with no idea what to expect of her time at the Ashram. What have each of them made of their stay?

Alex spent just over a week at the Ashram before leaving to do some travelling in southern India. "It took me three days to get over my exhaustion," he says. "I didn't give myself any time between arriving in India and coming to the Ashram, so I was jet-lagged and moody for a while – I felt confused and I couldn't get into it all." But he says that this soon passed. "Once I'd normalised my sleeping and got used the early morning waking up, I was fine."

Alex found learning about the teachings to be the most interesting aspect of his stay. "The lectures were the best part," he says. "Learning about the philosophy, what to do and not to do in order to achieve spiritual progress and lead a healthy life – it was exactly what I'd hoped I'd learn about. It was much better than reading all this from a book because at the Ashram we are actually leading the life prescribed – I'd describe it as a kind of 'lived-learning'." Alex says that he now feels more reverential towards life's ordinary routines. "What I've realised," he says "is that spiritual learning demands action. It isn't enough to read books about religion or philosophy or spirituality, unless you are prepared to put into action what you have learned. I've seen that spirituality can be at the heart of even the most mundane of everyday tasks. One small example: eating meals in silence with an attitude of grace. Another example: looking for opportunities to offer help with no thought for personal gain."

Alex says that one of the biggest lessons for him was combining care of the spiritual life with care of the body. "I'd never given much thought to that, but it makes sense," he says. In this respect, Alex valued the asana practice. "The yoga was good. I don't think I'll go as far as some as a practitioner, but I now realise that neglecting the body in favour of the intellect is counter-productive. We are a total system and we need to care about all the working parts – from physical to spiritual."

Maria had planned a two-week stay at the Ashram, and she stayed for the full period before leaving to meet up with her boyfriend in Goa. For her, it was the asana practice that was most inspiring. "What we learned in the lectures was interesting and the *satsang* was fun, but what I really loved was the yoga." Maria says that her body feels stronger and more supple and that she has almost mastered the Scorpion pose - a challenge she set herself at the start of her stay. However, she also found that she'd discovered something deeper in her practice. "One thing I'll take away with me is that yoga is so much more than perfecting the postures. Previously I'd been concerned with my degree of flexibility and in learning new variations. Now I see that I need to go more deeply into each posture. I've realised that I can find a peace there which reflects a growing peace within myself. I've found a beauty in this that I wasn't expecting."

Maria – already a vegetarian - says that she is now interested in learning more about the *sattvic* diet. "The philosophy behind the diet is interesting," she says. "I'm keen to see whether I can incorporate the way of eating into my life at home." Maria's new-found interest goes further than the food. "One of the lectures was given by an Ayurvedic doctor," she says. Ayurveda is the ancient traditional Indian science of medicine. "As a nurse, I know about how the body works but this really intrigued me. It seems like a very natural way to work with the body. I'm seriously thinking of taking a course in Ayurvedic medicine when I get home." Maria sums up her time at the Ashram: "I've arrived at a physically and mentally healthier, more peaceful place."

The Ashram, its practices and teachings have helped and encouraged thousands of people from all over the world to open their hearts and their minds to the ancient teachings of yoga as taught by Swami Vishnudevananda and his teacher Swami Sivananda and to take away with them something of profound value. Not everyone who comes responds in the same way – as we've seen from the stories of those who have shared their experiences, the effects that the Ashram and its teachings are as varied as the people who come here. Not all would describe themselves as spiritual seekers and not all arrive at the same spiritual place at the end of their stay. Some certainly have a clear aim or purpose in visiting. Some know that they are seeking something but are unsure what. Others find the Ashram by chance. Many sense something of value straight away, while some leave before fully committing themselves to the principles taught at the Ashram. Whatever your thoughts, feelings and views, whether you see yourself as a seeker or not, the advice given by the Ashram's visitors is consistent: Be curious, be open, try everything.

Om Shanti

Author's acknowledgements

I am greatly indebted to Nataraj, Director of the Sivananda Yoga Vedanta Dhanwantari Ashram, who understood and shared my vision of presenting the experiences of the Ashram's visitors, and who has facilitated the publication of 'Ashram'. I also extend my profound and most humble thanks to all the contributors: visitors to the Ashram who so willingly and openly shared their stories with me. I am certain that future visitors will find something of value in the experience and advice given with such open hearts.

Om Namah Sivaya

About the author

Hazel Manuel is a Paris based, UK-born writer. She has travelled extensively in India and visits the Sivananda Yoga Vedanta Dhanwantari Ashram on a regular basis. Swami Sivananda's teachings have not only had a positive impact on Hazel's life and her beliefs, but have also inspired her novels, which seek to explore spiritual concerns within a contemporary context. You can learn more about Hazel and her work at her website: www.hazelmanuel.net

'Ashram' was written as a karma yoga offering in thanks and gratitude to the Ashram and its staff, and to the teachings of Swami Sivananda and Swami Vishnudevananda.

Printed in Poland
by Amazon Fulfillment
Poland Sp. z o.o., Wrocław